THE O...

THE K ...... OF
LOVE

by Amy Mandeville

Illustrations by Kourtney Harper

Nightingale

An imprint of Wimbledon Publishing Company
LONDON

Copyright © 2000
Illustrations © 2000 WPC

First published in Great Britain in 2000
by Wimbledon Publishing Company Ltd
P.O. Box 9779 London SW19 7ZG
All rights reserved

First published 2000 in Great Britain

ISBN: 1903222 09 5

Produced in Great Britain
Printed and bound in Hungary

You change the sheets for cool, smooth fresh ones. You light a few scented candles, wear perfume and use talcum powder. You change into unlikely underwear. You've just completed a love ritual.

Call it love, call it lust, call it marriage, every culture has a means by which it standardises and then customises the way in which a man and a woman will meet to mate and procreate. It's like eating, breathing and sleeping. It keeps us alive and keeps us going. But like all of our other basic survival processes, we humans like to shroud it in myth, ritual and good manners. While many of the rituals and customs in the book will seem odd, perhaps even cruel, a roll in the hay without the requisite ritual would be rude in the extreme. This book will tell you when and where you're supposed to hit your bride over the head with a shoe and how it is sometimes appropriate to worship your mother-in-law. It's a beautiful world out there.

Amy Mandeville
1999

In some parts of New Guinea, it is traditional for the bride to have sex during the wedding ritual with every man in her village to ensure fertility.

Newlyweds of the Dani tribe may go for as long as five years before having sex.

The Mangaian people of the Cook Islands believe that if you do not have sex three times a day you will go insane. It is up to the older women of the village to instruct younger men on how it's done.

Marriage between Inuits is arranged at birth but does not become official until they have sex. Once they do, they are considered officially married without any other ceremony having occurred.

An eastern European bride of Southern Slovakia on the Balkan Peninsula was at one time expected to remain a stranger to her husband, despite living with him and mothering his children. She would not approach him freely nor address him in public. She would be, however, allowed to converse freely with her husband's brothers, with the eldest of the brothers often becoming her best friend.

In some regions of Peru it is not uncommon for the bride to be de-flowered by her own mother in the presence of her future in-laws as proof of her purity.

In ancient Japan, where heavy eyebrows were considered to be one of a woman's greatest charms, the brows were shaved off at the time of marriage to symbolise the woman's subservience to her husband.

In ancient Ireland it was common for a man to give a woman a bracelet woven of human hair to symbolise their betrothal.

Before a wedding in Yugoslavia, men were once commonly shaved in public. Every hair of his beard was then gathered, wrapped in a towel and given to his bride.

A Turkish wedding lasts for three days, during which time everyone participates in the party except for the bride, who remains in seclusion.

In Gloucester at the beginning of the 18th century it was traditional to break a large cake over the head of the bride and groom.

The word 'honeymoon' comes from the Northern European custom of the bridal couple drinking mead (made from honey) for the duration of a month (a moon).

In the north of England, it was at one time customary for one of the oldest residents of the neighbourhood to throw a plateful of shortbread over the bride's head.

In ancient Britain, a father gave his new son-in-law one of his daughter's shoes to symbolise the marriage. The bride was then informed of this transaction by being hit over the head with the shoe.

Amongst some tribes in India it is common to say 'smell me' when asking for a kiss.

In England it was at one time common for a woman to live with a man until she fell pregnant, at which point they married. Many years passed without a single illegitimate child being listed in the records, and there were very few childless married couples.

In many parts of the world, kissing was unknown until it was introduced by western explorers.

Among the Banyankoles of Central Africa, when a couple visit another couple, it is traditional to swap partners for the duration of the visit.

In Eastern Tibet it was at one time considered lucky for a foreigner to have sex with your wife.

In Scotland of old it was the pastor's inalienable right to kiss the bride immediately after the ceremony. It was felt that the happiness of the couple depended on it.

Some Eskimos still wife-swap as a matter of course. This is particularly true if a man is going on a long trip and has a wife who is too old or pregnant to go with him. He will instead bring along the younger, childless wife of a friend.

At one time, in some North American tribes, husband and wife never left their family homes, the children staying with their mother. The only thing spouses shared was their bed at night.

In Caracas, if a man takes a fancy to a woman he tells her so and then goes with her to her home. If she then offers him water to bath himself, and food to eat, they are considered married until such a time as she throws him out.

In medieval times, couples were sometimes made to settle marital arguments with a duel. The man stood in a hold while the woman was permitted to stand free above him. Both held a stout club, and whoever won was considered justified by the court.

Among the Khari tribe of Assam, men are courted by women and are expected to make a great show of vigorous resistance, followed by flight. When he is finally captured he is led to the nuptial residence amid great lamentation from his parents, and is considered married.

Feudal lords in Europe had the right to command any man over eighteen and any woman over fourteen to marry.

According to feudal law, a groom would invite his landlord and his lady to his wedding. The landlord was expected to bring the gift of a cartload of wood and his wife was required to supply a quarter of a roast pig. When the wedding was over, the landlord would either sleep with the bride or be compensated by the groom to the measure of five shillings and a sixpence.

Among the Zulus, the first wife purchased diligently helps her husband to raise the funds to purchase a second wife, who is then accorded a lower status than the first wife.

At one time, among some native Californians, men not only married an entire group of sisters, but also the sisters' widowed mother.

Among the Araucanians of Chile, the groomsmen used to barter a bride price with the father of the bride, while the groom sneaked into the house and captured his bride. Once they had reached the forest, they were considered married.

Monogamy only occurs in about 16% of societies, with only a third of these wholly disapproving of extra-marital sex.

In the Congo a man will capture his bride and then take her with him into the forest while he hunts for game. Should she become pregnant he keeps her with him until the child is weaned, at which point he takes the wife back to the village along with half the game he has captured in return for the child.

Among the Mosquito Indians the groom would carry off the bride while being followed by her women kinfolk who would stage a mock battle pretending to rescue her. The couple would then escape and go into hiding for the requisite amount of time.

Among the Koryak tribe of Siberia, a bride will have her friends sew her a chastity garment before she is scheduled to be 'captured' by her groom. The groom then attacks her at the appropriate time while she resists according to custom. The groom then, pressing his physical advantage, takes out a knife and cuts loose her chastity garment and reaches inside to touch her genitals. It is at this point that the couple are considered married.

A distinction is made between wives and concubines in Muslim countries. The Koran allows four wives, and as many concubines as a man can support.

In some cultures, including that of the Natchez tribe of Louisiana, it was once customary for a girl to prostitute herself to raise the money for her dowry.

According to Jewish custom, a widow had to marry her husband's brother if her first husband had not provided her with a son. If a son was then born from the union with the brother, he was named after the woman's first husband and considered his son. A man who did not wish to marry his brother's widow was then required to publicly remove his shoe and have it spat upon.

Amongst the Brahmin, men were not allowed to get married before their elder brothers. If a younger brother wanted to marry, however, and there was not a prospective bride for the older brothers, the older brothers would often marry a tree, thus freeing the younger sibling to marry.

The Punjab of India were traditionally superstitious of a twice-widowed man marrying a third time. Hence, when it was time to take a third bride, he would instead wed a tree or sheep that had been dressed in the clothing of his third bride while the woman sat nearby. It was felt that any evil spirits that wished the wife of the man ill would then be fooled into persecuting the tree or sheep instead.

The Mongols permitted a woman to marry four brothers - three to go to war and one to stay behind with her.

The marriage ritual of the Garo of Asia proceeds like this: the priest gets a fowl and then holds it in his left hand as he gives light blows to the back of the bride first and then the groom. The head is torn off the fowl. The priest then gets another fowl and gives blows first to the groom and then to the bride. The head of this fowl is then torn off. This indicates that the bride and groom have become husband and wife for the rest of their lives.

Amongst Australian aborigines, it is said a prospective groom would stalk a neighbouring tribe and, finding a woman who took his fancy, would hit her over the head with a club and drag her away. Once she had been revived the man would force her to follow him to his tribe where he raped her in front of witnesses as a symbol of their marriage.

Until the late eighteenth century, marriages were based on capture, purchase or barter instead of romance. Romance was restricted to extramarital affairs.

The Todas of India married in groups: say, six sisters and six brothers. The paternity of a child was determined by birth order. The first child of each wife belonged to the eldest brother, while the second belonged to the second eldest and so on.

In the past, Peruvians would encourage trial marriages and took a dim view of chastity. If a marriage failed, it was the woman who was blamed for not having learned enough about pleasing a man sexually before marrying.

The African Baganda, Bagishu and Suaheli tribeswomen used to stretch the inner labia so that they would hang at least two inches below the vagina. This practice reportedly had its origin in the belief that if a girl masturbated a lot her labia would become extended. Men felt that these women had particularly healthy sex drives and married them first.

The Siwans of North Africa thought that if a man could slip his semen into the food of a woman he fancied then she would fall madly in love with him.

Among the Sirionos of Eastern Bolivia, lovers would spend hours grooming one another - picking lice from their hair and wood ticks from their bodies and eating them. They removed worms and spines from their skin, glued feathers to their hair and then covered their faces with paint.

The Swedish Lapps felt that if you mixed a few drops of your blood with a drink given to your beloved then they would come to desire you.

Amongst the Serbs in Europe, it was believed that a girl could charm a young man by looking at him through the wing of a bat or through the ring of a dead person.